SELF PORTRAIT AS A CUP AND SAUCER

Fred Duignan

Introduction, by Andy Clausen

Silver Hollow Press I Chichester, New York

ACKNOWLEDGEMENTS

I would like to express deep gratitude to my poetry
mentors without whom I would not have found my way

Jim Klein
Michael O'Brien
Geoffrey Nulle
Tom DePoto
Bob Quatrone

ISBN 978-0-9989568-1-7

First Edition

Cover Art by Fred Duignan
Cover Design by Nathalie Andrews
Illustrations by Fred Duignan

Silver Hollow Press
265 Silver Hollow Road
Chichester, New York 12416-5129

for Sara and Zack

INTRODUCTION

by Andy Clausen

I knew of Fred Duignan from his paintings, which I liked. My art appreciation skills are unschooled, and I have a Plebian manual laborer's affinity for representational art. I enjoyed them even though most of his work would be classified as abstract. In it, I saw people, objects and spirits that for many were not easy to see, and I was excited by the emotional intensity.

Occasionally, Fred would come to open poetry readings and recite one or two of his poems. I mused, "Hey, he's pretty good." Well, I was wrong. He is very good. Terrific. His employment of descriptive language & his ability to reach and communicate universal personal feeling is superlative.

There are five sections in this book, and they differ in feel & form. SELF PORTRAIT AS A CUP AND SAUCER begins with the section Self Portrait in which the first poem *So Long Lady* reveals a great sadness, his love for women is undeniable and yet he seeks comfort in the places of fruitless expired love. *Duncan's Reach* expresses that theme again.

> "The scent of her left
> on this blanket
> traveled the white lines one way
> to the blue sea"

The relationship to the baby cared for in the work *Zack* seems to suggest he is the boy's father. The brilliant work *Carafe* proposes that we were happier way back when,

> "The inside of a crystal wine glass
> will entertain the explosion
> leading to the fall of civilization
> and the time of angels..."

4

"Time will exist like an eternal red
under the land
Where the old symbols are replaced..."

" Love with bleached bones
flags with airhorns
and the cross with an exposed nerve"

I find remarkable vividness in the piece *I Am a Racist,* a splendid and moving work whose ending is super. It is compelling but the racist part is built on a false paradigm (I believe by writer's intention) that a racist can be such by birth. I believe racism is an act of will and is taught and infused. Racism without instructors & like cohorts expires. And Fred is anything but a racist.

Then comes the moving poem *Dad* accomplishing a stab to the heart that moistened the unseen part of my seeing orbs till they leaked. In another world, imagine what could have been. This one recognizes what was, what happened.

The honesty, the language apt, fluid and often surprising impresses a classic deep love/ less than admiration, relationship. Even if the remainder of the poems were pedestrian (which they are not) this poem would stand out worthy of purchase.

Next a section entitled Short Poems where the poems are short but long in thought. Some squeeze the forehead into crenelated furrows, others inaugurate a smile at a twisted corner of mouth as they invoke religious parables. One does not utter, "huh?" at the end of any of these, clarity is paramount.

A tall boy between my legs
chills the cool
of friends bloated with their fullness of "see?"
traveling across my sizzling skin.
Heat nipping at my ankles
where the darkness remains
I crush the empty can.

In the following section Cup, he realizes why he paints: to find out universal secrets. In *Paint Is an Animal*, paint is indeed an animal, a wild hand trying to control a horse ridden by a determined Cossack collaborator.

"Paint is an animal
fiery of purpose yet poised.
Mating in its own liquid, guiding the journey
ignoring all rules
unafraid."

In Looking at this Cup of Paint, Duignan writes about paint preparation,

"Shaping liquid in a four-walled
eloquent circle
believing in sudden know-it-all jolts
that are ravenously endless..."

Milwaukee Cadaver is hard & brutal the way reality seems to be as of late.

"When we reached the uterus
the professor smiled.
Opening the organ, she held up
a baseball sized object.
"Tumors all over."

Martha's vagina was sewn shut.
Martha committed suicide."

Marker is a portrait of one who worked to make life better, especially in our future.

"Intelligent in the ways of instinct
Determined by the snarl of passion
and carefully loved

for honesty and listening
to the second thoughts
of his tugging heart...

There's no business like no business
when land of mind and air of freedom
are threatened.
At this lowest moment he remains
reminding all of what he knew
we have."

The description in *Young Poet* is quite familiar to the poets that participate in the "poetry scene" from NYC to Kathmandu, from Bisby, Arizona to Albany, New York from Woodstock to Seattle: another possible Rimbaud brazen, energetic and tenderfoot silly.

"Fuck, fuck, fuck, fuck, fuck!
I'm so suicidal
That I drank the pink liquid
held in the mouth of an ex-junkie
out to prove his rehabilitation
in private
My skin pales in the end
Art Sucks, Art Sucks, Art Sucks!"

The first stanza of *MUD* is an accurate recounting of the extremes of his artist's personality not a smooth 60 mph but 20 backwards and three digits forward, the mind returning to simple & eloquent beauty of the bed yet smacked by the arduous and even deracinating "mud up to my knees"

...a powder blue blanket
on top of pure white sheets
stained with Mother's blood
torn clothes and
forced sex.

The CODA of the final long poem *3Twenty9* is a powerful elegy. of his father and mother's deaths.

As I write this, I understand one must read his work to appreciate what I'm saying about it. If one likes language of confessionary truth, empathetic vigor & visionary imagination SELF PORTRAIT AS A CUP AND SAUCER delivers.

Fred's fervor and eye complimenting description wills to see it through. Where one decides to express what is seen and felt with paint and words, one doesn't let looming Death control the actions, doesn't let Death control the words that become action.

Duignan's book is not for those that want page after page of description of a cat's antics or a pretty piece of paper or strange syntax one treats like a word game in their verse. This is a painter/poet confronting self and his internal as well as external public take on the world and his devotional love.

Contents

SELF PORTRAIT

SHORT POEMS

CUP

SAUCER

3TWENTY9

SELF PORTRAIT

So Long Lady

(for Susan)

I can see her in a long
black dress singing a Blues
ballad to the floating dreams
of the sounds
as I the piano player
who loves her
slowly move my hands
up and down the keys.

The lipstick stained glass,
trophy for another lover
lost for her inconsistency of
thoughts clouded in the ice
tides of her body
reflects her flame inside
itself to discover the little girl
that wanted to be
denied
picked
wilting
before the water filled vase
unsure of the effects.

Now, I have lost my fingers
walking the Mission on Easter
sharing a liquid story
with brokenhearted sailors
who sit in future construction sites.

They warn me of the bitch
with the demon eyes,
killing men again and again
they are found with her
throwing bottles at images
in granite slabs.

I have difficulty understanding
such passion, trying to suppress
the indulgence and sorrow
watching the sunset
wondering if Jesus went
back to the tomb.

Pity the irony of a Holy Thursday
consumption like a white vision
that held my future
in those soft hands.
Her heartbeat came and hovered
above the San Francisco Bay
interrupted by the prayers
of rushing traffic.

Duncan's Reach

Watch me care deeply
like a butterfly pinned for display
as my freefalling mind
screams
I can be King.

See my hand holding onto
the transparent disk
that lights up and loops
into "Rock the Cradle"
between a triangle of string
swinging like my personal gallows.

The wavering passion--
as human faults are released
by my sleep, each dream
depicting chaos.

Between the layers of skin
the spirit speaks of the way
soaring folds
my clothing of her body
wet with last night's kiss.

The scent of her left
on the blanket
traveled the white lines one way
to the blue sea
balancing my experiences
of a dozen betrayals
with hope
that she would thrust
beyond sex
toward the value in
the trustworthy embrace of eyes.

Zack

You arrived mouth first
echoing inside your mother
the moment they cut the fourth
Caesarian line
in her democratic skin.

And you wouldn't shut up.
Recklessly screaming at kind practitioners
who cleaned your body,
making you look like a human
instead of a glazed donut.

Even when they tried to
suck the goo out of your vibrato
you complained which
made me imagine that maybe
you didn't like being here or
that you needed to tell me
some secret about your last
eight months and twenty-four day
sentence in the hole.

Apgar perfection mitigated
my fear of a hangover
and withdrawal offered
by a person I never knew
really couldn't imagine existed
when we laid naked in the dunes
outside the Ferguson house.

We added quartz to our juices
and slept before being
stirred and awakened by the
pump pump pump
of a new machine valve.

Finally, a masked woman
silenced you
as she put my finger in your mouth
freeing me to give up part of my flow
as you sucked.

Carafe

The inside of a cut crystal wine glass
will entertain the explosion
leading to the fall of civilization
and the time of angels.
No new ideas will sprout then
only the loneliness of November days
that lose voice to the hum of regret.

New ash clouds
will need a reason to drive them
across the sky
to meet rain
over new continents
replenishing
the fluid in the eyes
of corrupt men who ended on top.

That generation of artists
will use the shells of extinct species
as communicating coils
to children watching holographic images
of trees, clean water and real food.

Time will exist like an eternal red
under the land
where the old symbols are replaced:
Love with bleached bones
flags with air horns
and the cross
with an exposed nerve

Bad Thinking

The fan above me spins
like a manic clock
as I look for unnamed
supplements that firm up
weak intentions.
Pain travels so slowly
as I seek the experience of joy
within my deeper self
now collecting dust.

When imagination is left unbridled
like a child's vision
the future and its promise are born.

I am too worn out to fight for it.
One foot in front of the other
has tripped me up
and age has swallowed my faith
that tomorrow offers a better chance
to reclaim my birthright again
for the first time.

Today I believe it is time to at least
give up.

And So We Learn

Crib crying
hungry, lonely, afraid
until elevation
brings us to arms, nipple and warmth
easing the dread
caressing the brow.

And so we learn

Resting in the wake of
child's play nightmares
where the
smell of whiskey and Old Spice
mingle in the aroma of ritual
like a midnight raid on
Zorro's hat and rapier.

And so we learn

Accelerating
toward the wall of what did I do--
Why not?
it felt good
until truly undone
by aftermath, touchstones
the mirror's reflection.

And so we learn

If disciplined, conscious, lucky
fallen folly fades
revealing opportunity
to achieve, produce
or maintain
within the world's view
our own imaginings
righteousness.

And so we learn

Silent images of shadows
both loving and neutral
mouthing goodbyes as
blackness beckons
the end
end
it's not true
I'm not finished
not now
not yet

it can't--

And so_____

I Am a Racist

I am a racist by birth
in line with history, media and
white fear.
There were no interactions
to measure by as a 7-year old
in 1959 suburbia.
Nothing but dad's decree
at the kitchen table
warning of crime, laziness
job loss and predatory lives.

In 1963 the Black and White TV
opened a dialogue between us.
Pleading logic ended with
threats and anger
fear and silence
in line with the images
of non-violent men and women
beaten, fire hosed
and dog mauled.

Four years later, on a moon bright
wet street night we rode together.
He without question, I filled with doubt
until traffic stopped us suddenly.
My father exited
running toward chaos at the crossroads.

Defying his words to stay put
I straddled the line of vehicles
as a frightened 15-year-old
until I witnessed him leaning his fist
on the chest of a bleeding black man
lying next to a twisted motorcycle.

Trying to calm the shaking body
blacktop covered in blood
that flowed to the sewer grate
he called him
"buddy"
"pal"
"son"
until the trembling stopped
the rider stiffened
and my father wept.

Dad

I'm sittin' here sippin' on bourbon.
It's been a long time. I can't
remember when I've been so together. He said I'd only be
hurting myself.
I don't believe I'm gonna do this.

Dog was chasing his tale
loved it, I told it.
Played Jesus the night
I got on my knees and told him
we all loved each other
next night said I'd make him howl.
Next day told him
I was a liar.
Wanted him crushed.

Life makes fantasies real.
I live them, eat them.
It's why people ask who I'm talking to
who I'm waving at
always a gin mill.
I am 3.

My father was dying of cancer.
He used to turn off the heat.
I got used to falling
asleep to the sound of my chattering.
He carried a can of gasoline around
with him all the time.
He tempted God to come
down and face him.

The next morning
he was beaten to a pulp.
Next week his biopsy will be positive.
I started to believe again.
Up to now I was Stephen Dedalus.

It's now 7/17/73 or 4. I don't remember. I should look
at the memorial card I took at the wake,
I'm not sure it will be there.
I may be free. Let's wait till this is over.

In tears I said he should be washed
he was my father.
I was proud.
I slung him over my shoulder.
He almost fell in the toilet,
but I caught him by the pelvic bone.
The water was nice and warm.
I stood him up – ankles high,
the white flakes of filth gushed
up violently with the bubbles
by his ear.
His right hand moved enough
to knock a cake
of Ivory soap into the bath.
It floated over to the neckline.

I took him out,
put him in his bed,
dried his loose body,
looked in his eyes as he said, "please,"
and went to my deli job.

I tried slicing my fingers off
but the customers kept saying "no
ends please."

That night had to take him to the hospital
he wasn't too good.

Waited for me instead of God
to come home and dress him.
He handed me his hat first
I must take after him.
It turned out even worse.
I called the ambulance.

Emergency Room white
on the bed trying to breath,
saw me,
laughed,
waved,
the nurse pulled the curtain
in front of him.

To the sobs of my people
I dated a girl that night.
Married her.
I had to do penance.

I knew who you were
the day you said my poem lied.
I tried so hard to prove
you unworthy.
I got what I wanted.

SHORT POEMS

Williams' Plums

Williams' plums have all been eaten
leaving room for this stoic ripe pear.
Now out of the deep freeze
soft and sweet
accepting the role of first heir
to a history spotted by a lack of kindness
tossed brutally around the plate
reviving its mandate to juicy blindness
refusing the comfort of hate.

A Note

A note on the keyboard displays
your signature style in type
as the stain of sweat left on the pillow
reminds me of the curve of your neck
like a road offering a journey
to new lands.

Stranded

Standing on an island
neither kindness nor lifeboat in sight
water calm and ultimately beautiful
glistens with reflections that graciously invite
a gaze so intent on spying
protection from a distant shore
when standing right behind you
is what you want and a little bit more.

Sun

Sunday sweat runs down my face,
scorching your cheeks
as the heat snakes
from the top of my head
to your sandals
cooling the stone steps.

What glory this sunflower of a day?

You answer with your usual whisper,
that enters my dry ear.
There is wisdom in this desert,
that teaches me lessons once again.
Knowing that it can all end if I will but move my tongue
across your lips.

Dancing Tonight

Dancing tonight in what is claimed as a new world,
the fear of drowning fades as the
women compete
for their place as immortal goddesses
within each other's eyes.

Reminded of a poet friend's image of liquid thighs I dive
head-first into
the waters once more.

Formal Sadness

The winding lines are not just the space they inhabit
shadows of scraping and wash.
Through, within and above them
courses life, energy, purpose
that follows the outer to influence
the inner.

Their edges are refuge for all
and the space between conduits
that carry the socialization
between entities, filling the void
with sound that follows them from invisibility to immobility,
drawing a space that depicts lives lived.

What Next?

Proper response depends on the song of the heart
where calm respects passion
after another new start has collapsed.

At this moment deep in the belly of knowledge and need
I compose a new song of desire.
Can one retain the truth of height across time?
With the book of remembrance beneath my feet, I continue
to climb.

Another Lifetime

Today is another lifetime
like a hiss inside my head.
New crimes are petty and useful
raising ambitions from the dead.

Like a mime that hands out great wisdom
without a word being spoken
there remains an unresolved feeling
like a vow this is unbroken.

Popular Cocktails in Parked Cars

Reading her words over wireless air
that wonder aloud about
time capsules waiting to be filled,
I watch the rain run down the windshield
waiting for an answer to appear.

A tall boy between my legs
chills the cool
of friends bloated with their fullness of "see?"
traveling across my sizzling skin.
Heat nipping at my ankles
where the darkness remains
I crush the empty can.

CUP

Painter

I do not want the power of
Michelangelo
nor the grace of
Raphael
like golden air that smells of smoke
from candles burning out loud.

It is the promise of secrets revealed
that seduces me,
allowing measure to provide
chorus and refrain
as tuneless delight.

Squeeze and push like
a mother in childbirth,
a beggar starving alone,
a one-handed lover.

Pour and brush
while particular-light embraces
my wit as the subject becomes a single thought,
unintelligible, developed outside of memory.

Slaughtering the result
gaining new insight
as to the truth in wardrobe
like the naked Emperor
clothed with innovation,
almost avant-garde.
I step-dance with joy
naked and ritual-less.

Painting #1

Painting the canvas that forever recalls
the nights lost in madness of our passionate falls.
When the dark invades where light used to be
and takes its rightful place
outside of destiny.

Quince and powder shower my mind
with memories of color
carried through time.

Rolling along with another idea
toasting the moment
with a cup of fear
before the canvas helps me understand
there is a-very-fast line
in the palm of my hand.

Studio Love

Remember when we rolled up together
into the canvas on the floor?
A painting of epic nudes in love
hidden behind the open door.

Spilling my joy, color, and light
on wrinkled fabric stained with hue
smiling impressions drawn in close
the most gently lightened and beautiful blue.

From Inside Orange

Limpid and languishing
I call for beginnings
that end before
sinewy muscle can respond.

It is the fruit of action
desperate and incarnate
in search of words
to explain
where and why this is
needed.

Grappling within this field,
totality listens for my retort
that can only be heard
with medium eyes and
the knowledge of intuition.

Look!
there it isn't
feeding on delicious light
falling face down
on top of the surface.

Paint is an Animal

Thank you for your interest
at this demonstrative moment of choice when smell and
touch mix
with vision, lack of thought
(barrier to focus)
and cleared paths, ending in another collaboration.

Paint is an animal
fiery of purpose yet poised.
Mating in its own liquid, guiding the journey
ignoring all rules
unafraid.

Can you give me a hint?

There is length during trailblazing
quarantined in light and shape
idea and surface
that requires swallowing,
immersion
cleanliness, filth and belief
resulting in space.

I execute aloud in response
to my eye settling
upon this exact time
that finishes at top speed
recumbent in pools
on chaotic surface
before it finds where to be.

As my schooling pulls
at my balls
I kick out of those ties
that tame
and break the spirit of color, light and form with technique
and style.

Instead I swim in ultramarine
slide across crimson
and soar in the glow of cadmium
arriving at a place that lathers,
frustrates, teases and relents
until arriving
in the company of others
who's pictures
reside on walls
public, private,
no more.

Looking at this Cup of Paint

Those who have not
the whole toward, truly
clamor down the empty corridor
strangely authoritative.

Shaping liquid in a four-walled
eloquent circle
believing in sudden know-it-all jolts
that are ravenously endless
by way of first principles
until it spills.

SAUCER

Escape Plan

The raft that promises escape
to a pure and simple place
must first be dragged through wet
gray industrial stained topsoil
that hides black mud underneath
through swamp grass and rising
cattails to the stagnant water's edge.

On both sides of the watercourse
released smoke
huge oil tanks with
ladders running up their sides
dot one's vision.
Steel and concrete buildings
house momentless thinking
all illuminated by refinery gas torches
signaling authoritarian rule
encased in barrels of crude
wealth's primacy
and acts of cruelty
bringing new meaning to
the shouts of blood and soil.

When the lifeboat is ready for release
into the creek where gasoline greens, pinks and blues
swirl like a psychedelic light show
the raft realizes it is but a broken palate
that carried goods to market
full of cost savings slots
that will not float.

That Morning
(for Elizabeth)

In the new light
your focused squint
seemed to recognize the mind
I attempted to season before offering it
to the arena.

Remembering
the night I opened your floodgates
I finally found a subject for
the poem that arrived after your body
was returned to Wales.

"It felt like a Sunday in Brooklyn
at The River Café with the sky-scraping
Catskills watching as
you smiled genuinely
over bites of omelette and the Mediterranean Esopus
churned muddy
with the sound of Spring runoff."

Obituary

Did they get it right?
You found nothing along the way
that gave you pleasure
except gaining more.

Did you protect the treasury
with refusal to see the
hungry strangers
standing next to you?

Can mercy erase their guilt
for not having the ability, luck or legacy
you possessed?

Will the big Ledger in the Sky
bless your efforts of maintaining
a life in the black?

So, when the gold melts
from your wrist, neck, ankles and earlobes
to return to the earth
tell me
was it price or value?

Remember
(for Gary)

I pushed through the crowd, into a room
filled with sixteen black wooden boxes.
On their lids were torn garments.
I didn't understand.

Someone directed me
to one of the crates in the corner.
On its lid of blinding fuchsia
were two gold masks
contorted and clever.
I opened it.
I could see the man inside
was not content.

From behind,
a woman approached.
Saying I'm sorry for your trouble.
She said he was a ventriloquist
who'd lost his puppet. She feared
he could not be saved.

We sat in mourning for seven days
while his friends came
one by one.
They treated us
to varied soft-shoe
one-liner, slapstick
routines.

As the last performer exited
the woman turned to wood.
I placed her
in his arms and received
a standing ovation.

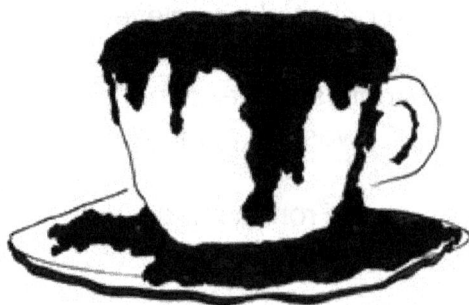

Milwaukee Cadaver

The instructor opened her head
like a walnut
holding up Martha's Brain.
The imagination was hidden inside,
motor abilities all surface.

Martha's flopping breasts
laid beside her open ribs.
Our guide smiled as she ended the myth
once and for all,
"they're only fat."

Martha's muscles were taut
as we were led through the large and small intestines.
When we reached the uterus
the professor smiled.
Opening the organ, she held up
a baseball sized object.
"Tumors all over."

Martha's vagina was sewn shut.
Martha committed suicide.

"We don't tell our students histories."

Marker

He Lived through war
like a tree scorched
by fire and struck by lightening

Gnarled by empty demands
moved with subtle handling
followed closely
as a danger to what some believed
was obvious.

Intelligent in the ways of instinct
Determined by the snarl of passion
and carefully loved
for honesty and listening
to the second thoughts
of his tugging heart.

That voice remains
as a thunderous dictum
to all who would rally
around the prosperity
that some have been waiting for.

There's no business like no business
when land of mind and air of freedom
are threatened.
At this lowest moment he remains
reminding all of what he knew
we have.

Compact

The smell of an empty
lip gloss container and a metal square
revealing a colored hole fully centered
with its lid
folded back
forming a right angle
huddle in a leather purse.

She covers her body with
rubber cement
for vanity
until it shines
spreads and feels its own weight.

On our anniversary
it will stick as the body binds
and the mind revolts
remembering the time spent
trapped within painted bubbles.

Purgatory
(For George)

You told me of a place
between Heaven and Hell
distant
in a corner
separated from light,
far from perfect
stretched, twisted
for the moment
until the gate cracks
and the threat of death ends.

Furious at the fallen
who lied that all are lost
but them,
you remained
hopeful, desperate
decent
forged in fire
cleansed with virtue
tempered by pain.

A gracious silence
reasons it through
plucking captives wearily
roused
from their blindness
revealing the light
of Love.

We Can Be Famous Someday

Strong words oppose my blue streak
intriguing your twice divorced mind
blinding the wink
between the curls.

The ongoing tic-tac-toe games
on the walls of unisex heads
in sheet metal do wop halls
are our backdrop.

I stall in double jeopardy
while you give the next ex
a victory
that places us on the unlisted.

Our problems come
in threes. We only have the phone
number on the mirror
and not enough cash for the night.

But we'll look good in print.

Our faces blazing in porcelain fireplaces
while watching from an open skylight
at stagnant pools reflecting our humanity
like orange lights
in the anesthetized stare
of your eyes.

Young Poet

One eye rolls up
the other sideways
as he approaches the microphone
of his inner auditorium
littered with rags.

Blue ones tied in knots. Pink ones
wrapped around steam pipes.
White ones pasted to walls with
some other culture's blood.

"Fuck, fuck, fuck, fuck, fuck,
I'm so suicidal
that I drank the pink liquid
held in the mouth of an ex-junkie
out to prove his rehabilitation
in private.
My skin pales with the end.
Art Sucks, Art Sucks, Art Sucks!"

The great mind remains
in the warmth of his success
left by the admiring audience
that left him with an empty tub
of popcorn and a pool of black coffee
at the bottom of a paper cup
revealing a crushed, filtered Kool
held in place
by a melted cherry
lollipop.

Mud

My mind is old
with dark terror hidden
under crocheted flowers
that cover a powder blue blanket
on top of pure white sheets
stained with mother's blood,
torn clothes and
forced sex.

Yesterday, color was freshly released
from deep damp brain
by fists pressed into blinded eyes
while looking for the truth of the street
to inform the triumph of art.

There's mud up to
my knees
and some crazy bird
drawing breath from my confusion.

Brown and crimson of feather
on a Spring night
without light or easy wind
to relieve this ache
another day closer to
answering the question of
the end
or anticipation of more
rings in my ears.

Like a song without sound
delight without fantasy
cradled in the light from her thighs
I remain
until the opposition calls "all in"
and this journey ends.

Until then, embracing time
I seek perfect pitch
in the music of fate.

3Twenty9

3Twenty9

There is no present or future, only the past, happening
over and over again, now.
Eugene O'Neill, A Moon for the Misbegotten

I

My Mother's Heart
beat in time with
the tubercular cough
of a dying father
determined dry Irish wit in
my grandmother's struggle
and a sister's love

At 3-years-old
she stood at a gate
shaking the bars of
"momma take me home" orphanage
before her "titter"
walked this prayer
back into the chapel
for Rosary
where she believed
they belonged

Bulova watch box
piece work
fueled
her adolescent independence
until
lips of deep red
fueled a fated night

of drinking and dancing where
she met him in a fog
produced by her hot sweat and
his cold need of a caretaker
for his dead wife's son

II

The Night my Father Split in Half
under a spurious moon
she sat on the floor
after being flung across the room
unaware of his break with
reality
of a red Normandy tide
swelling with the Okinawa Sea Bee's sting

His name was metaphor
duibh (black), gennain (a firbolg chief)
truck driver
green with Celtic pride
descended from Maine, 4th son of Niall
of the Nine Hostages

Son of an immigrant horse and wagon driver
and a defiant alcoholic mother.
Brother to a girl and four boys-
a Truckers' Union Official
a Brooklyn Dock Boss
and two who were murdered for their Labor
before being dumped
into the Hudson

Tonight

III

Kitchen Table
the royal seat of power
runs orange and white
hot with ham, mashed potatoes
and canned vegetables
digesting in stomachs
etherized with anticipation

Accused along wooden testimony
measured out in empty beer cans
an overflowing ashtray
and a pounding fist
like a gavel
on the sound block of family life
Father pushes the moment to a crisis
leading deliberations
based on no evidence and
created truths
until reaching a verdict
that is announced with a sudden –

IV

SLAM
The Mick hit #200
off Jim Bunning

Cheers!

SLAM
The front door opens to escape
the drunken shadow
carrying a red can of gasoline

Out!

SLAM
Mother's head dents
the living room's flowered wallpaper

Scream!

V

Dad's Desperate Descent Down
the damp cellar's steps
to his electronics repair workshop
where empty Philco and RCA TV cabinets
watch the Four Roses of his youth reappear

Illumination in the fire
of street corner metal barrel memories
billowing Lucky's smoke
his brother's
laughter, blasphemy and threats
emboldens his serenading
the seductive dancer
floating in the inky air
ripe with ancestor worship

VI

The Animal
is his primary voice.
Howling up the stairs
through the open cellar door
penetrating my racing ears
on all three landings
under bed covers
behind locked doors and
between coats in the hall closet
of the 3-story
pre-World War II era asbestos shingled
blue collar victory

VII

The Glowing Ember
of his cigarette
breathing in the darkness
was the face I knew
him by best

Like a Senufo fire spitter
designed to terrify
his 2nd born
fleeing open mouthed
up the stairs
from the cinder block room
held together with black electrical tape

Before re-emerging at the cellar door
he stumbles to the fuses that will be screwed
one half turn to the left
shutting off
the lights and furnace

VIII

Wire Taping Accuracy
was key to our relationship
black and red are hot
white is common

Stripping plastic with flame
and razor blades
we twisted the copper
tightly
in a relationship
designed to electrify
with no pain

But never cross the hot and common
Never cross the black and red with white

Do Not, no never
DO NOT!

IX

The Boy in the Zorro Mask
watches
the motherland mined
by the Lord of the land

As the defiler's idea
covers his eyes with
passionate hisses
he whets the cheek of
history's air
seeking revenge
as her calm watery blue
Caribbean vacation dream
gushes forth
from her body and mind

X

Pressing Childhood eyes
into fists
that dent the hard mattress
I proceed inward
to achieve silence

Color
light and form
dance with joy
or perhaps
run in terror
revealing the Wilderness
of my interior mythology
as prelude
to what is
now

XI

The Closed Cigar Box
retrieved once more by father
from the basement's highest
raw pine shelf
is a reliquary without hope

Naval service ribbons
live shells, am image
of shirtless men kneeling like altar boys
in front of heavy equipment
preparing for invading armies
and
the photograph of a woman
who is not my mother
dissolve this man back
into mud

XII

Smiles
Frowns and Tears
animate his memories
as this penitential act
grinds out of eyes
covered in death's shadow

The primary colors of the end
emerge as an inverse rainbow
coughing
within his cancerous mind
as he begs forgiveness

XIII

The Sun Rose over 3Twenty9
inevitably
ending the darkness
while leaving the remnants
of a mind stripped
to bone
that feared for our lives

XIV

Woman
alone after pushing
floor tile
carpet
mattress and couch away
stands
on shaking legs
strong with the conviction
that her children will never
hold onto
her orphan's iron gate
or call her name to be taken home

Coda

XV

Emergency Room White
on the bed trying to breathe
saw me
laughed
waved
the nurse pulled the curtain
in front of him

XVI

Laid to Rest
20 years later in the brown earth above him
her spirit finds peace
while his eyes and mouth
consume the last of her body

XVII

Flying across the globe
to a distant exhibition
I didn't make it to her funeral
like a stranger
by refusing a return ticket upon arrival

Paintings in the baggage compartment
seduced me with promise
while fueling escape
inherent within a pipe dream
like some drama I had to live

Fred Duignan

Fred Duignan began writing poetry as a young man in High School where he was wrongly accused of plagiarizing his first poem. He began publishing as a member of LUNCH, a poetry group that created a magazine by the same name as a non-student on the campus of Fairleigh Dickinson University in Rutherford, New Jersey.

Fred is a painter who graduated from the University of California Santa Cruz. He is a past Curator of Contemporary Art at the Paterson Museum in New Jersey and is a former art critic for COVER, a downtown NYC Arts & Entertainment Magazine.